CONTENTS

T0362758

ENGLISH BASICS.

PRE-TEST

Do this test before you start the book. It has been designed to test your ability in the areas this book will cover.

1 **Underline the noun from each of the following sentences.**

   a. The man stood still.
   b. The cat is black.
   c. My car is cool.
   d. Love is wonderful.

2 **Underline the pronoun from each of the following sentences.**

   a. We all love takeaways.
   b. I am tall.
   c. You can't say that.
   d. It stalks the corridors at night.

3 **Underline the adjective from each of the following sentences.**

   a. My dog is smelly.
   b. The water feels cold.
   c. The television is too loud.
   d. The food tasted disgusting.

4 **Underline the verb from each of the following sentences.**

   a. Mihirangi sings many songs.
   b. The dog chased the cat.
   c. I finished the dishes.
   d. The boy rode his horse.

5 **Underline the auxiliary verb from each of the following sentences.**

   a. I was sleeping.
   b. Mum can help you.
   c. She is feeling funny.
   d. I should eat less.

6 **Underline the adverb from each of the following sentences.**

   a. The horse runs fast.
   b. My mother cooks badly.
   c. Yesterday was hot.
   d. I can't find my peke anywhere.

7 **Underline the conjunction from each of the following sentences.**

   a. My brother and his friend had a quarrel.
   b. I had a shower because I was dirty.
   c. You can eat the leftover pizza but not the chips.
   d. I like to go walking although not when it is wet.

ISBN : 9780170462983

8 Underline the **preposition** from each of the following sentences.

a. My ball rolled under the table.

b. The plane soared above the town.

c. I flushed my fish down the toilet.

d. Most of an iceberg is beneath the water.

9 Put **capital letters** where needed.

a. my kuia is called aroha.

b. while watching the show, molly sneezed.

c. people call auckland the city of sails.

d. it doesn't matter which country you live in, the cities are all the same.

10 Put in an **apostrophe** where needed.

a. Mondays form meetings are always long.

b. The girls uniforms were messy.

c. I cant hear you.

d. Theyre supposed to go first.

11 Put in a **comma** where needed.

a. Before you go to bed brush your teeth.

b. Can we go see the tigers eat Mum?

c. If you love something set it free.

d. If it was yours it will return to you.

12 Put **speech marks** where needed.

a. What are you doing? demanded the policeman.

b. Nothing, replied the boy. I'm just looking.

c. The policeman glared. Are you being cheeky?

d. No, sir.

TO MARK YOUR WORK

Mark your answers using the Answers section. Each question has been scored out of 4.
The following is our assessment of your ability for each question:

4/4   Well done! You know and understand this topic.

3/4   Good work. You know what to do.

2/4   Not really good enough to say with confidence you understand what is needed.

1/4   You need to work on this topic.

COMMON NOUNS

A noun is a naming word.

Common nouns are nouns that refer to non-specific persons, places, objects or periods of time. For example: mother, student, kitchen, paddock, hat, house, century, week, cake, phone.

1 **Underline the common nouns in the following sentences.**

a. The dog wagged its shaggy tail.

b. The sailor threw the rope to the people on the boat.

c. The freshly cooked chocolate cake had been baked in the oven.

d. The student grabbed the encyclopaedia from the shelf to help with the research.

e. The mountain seemed huge as the people gazed from the lookout.

2 **Use the common nouns in the box below to complete the following passage.**

Shannon	beach	jandals	track	towel	rays
Shannon	creek	shed	Ashley	water	Ashley

_____ and _____ walked down the rutted

_____ to the _____. They passed the broken

utility _____ and jumped the farm _____.

_____ lay down on her _____ to catch

some _____ while _____ slipped off her

_____ and ran towards the cool, inviting _____.

3 **Now put your own nouns in to complete this passage.**

_____ placed his _____ against the _____.

He entered the cool _____ and after carefully investigating the

contents of the _____ he finally decided upon an _____.

The _____ was deep blue with brilliant gold _____.

He stepped out into the _____ and began to eat his smooth,

chilled _____.

PROPER NOUNS

Proper nouns are nouns that refer to a specific person, place, object or period of time.

Proper nouns are a special group of nouns that should always have a capital letter. They are as follows:

Names of people: Mr Jones, Whaea Tania, Russell, Fiona, Matua Tihirangi

Names of cities, towns and suburbs: Auckland, Ōtautahi, New Plymouth, Te Whanganui-a-Tara

Names of regions: North Island, South Island, Wairarapa, West Coast, Te Tai Rāwhiti

Names of countries: Aotearoa New Zealand, Australia, Taiwan, South Africa

Names of days of the week: Monday, Tuesday, Wednesday, Thursday, Rāpare, Rāmere...

Names of months of the year: January, February, March, April, ...

Names of organisations: Anglican Care Network, The Cancer Society

Names of titles: Sir Peter Jackson, Tā Tīmoti Karetu, Governor-General, Dr Baker

Names of important days: Waitangi Day, Boxing Day, Matariki, Labour Day

1 **Underline the proper nouns in the following sentences.**

   a. Mr Cottle caught the bus to Christchurch via Oamaru.

   b. Jason and Patrick were both starting their year at Avondale College.

   c. On Wednesday afternoon, Karen had a doctor's appointment.

   d. Connor had recently moved to New Zealand from Ireland.

   e. Waverley visited Te Papa while staying in Wellington.

2 **Circle where there should be capital letters in the following sentences.**

   a. We are going to taupō in the september school holidays.

   b. The waikato river flooded a lot of low-lying farmland last year.

   c. I had to visit dr mcbride at the starship children's hospital last monday.

   d. dame te atairangikaahu was māori queen for 40 years. In 2006, her eldest son, tuheitia paki, succeeded her after her death.

   e. My mother bought me hot cross buns on good friday and easter eggs for the sunday.

COLLECTIVE NOUNS

A collective noun is a noun that refers to a group or collection of similar people, animals or things.

Collective nouns are used when you want to refer to a whole group of people or objects but you don't want to call them all by their separate names. For instance, you wouldn't list all the members of a sports team in one sentence but rather you would call them a 'team'.

1 **Underline the** collective nouns **in the following sentences.**

a. The winning waka ama crew attended the charity dinner with their paddles.

b. A school of dolphins raced freely at the bow of the boat.

c. This year there will be national elections held to vote in our government.

d. There are fifteen people in a ki-o-rāhi team.

e. My parents had to go to a fundraising committee meeting at the marae.

2 **Choose, from the box below, the appropriate** collective noun **to complete the following phrases.**

colony	cluster	litter	choir	army
pride	gaggle	gang	bouquet	fleet

a. an _____ of soldiers

b. a _____ of ants

c. a _____ of flowers

d. a _____ of thieves

e. a _____ of lions

f. a _____ of stars

g. a _____ of ships

h. a _____ of puppies

i. a _____ of singers

j. a _____ of geese

ABSTRACT NOUNS

Abstract nouns refer to qualities or things that we cannot see. For instance: aroha, hate, hunger, humour.

1 Underline the abstract nouns in the following sentences.

a. Jenna's eyes were green with jealousy.

b. The corridors at school had an eerie quietness.

c. We have a dog called Tai. He shows loyalty to us.

d. Two thousand people marched up Queen Street to support world peace.

e. It is important there is honesty between friends.

You can change some words into abstract nouns by:
- adding 'ness' to the end; e.g. clever + ness = cleverness.
- adding 'ship' to the end; e.g. champion + ship = championship.
- adding 'hood' to the end; e.g. father + hood = fatherhood.

2 Change the following words into abstract nouns by adding 'ness'.

a. lonely _____   c. useless _____

b. happy _____   d. hopeless _____

3 Change the following words into abstract nouns by adding 'ship'.

a. friend _____   c. leader _____

b. owner _____   d. scholar _____

4 Change the following words into abstract nouns by adding 'hood'.

a. sister _____

b. neighbour _____

c. knight _____

d. child _____

PRONOUNS

Pronouns are used instead of nouns when referring to persons or things.

Pronouns are the last category of nouns that we will look at. The good thing about pronouns is that there is a limited number of them so once you've got them, you've got them! Pronouns have the same function as nouns and writers use them to save repeating a name too often in a sentence, passage or story. Below is a list of the most commonly used pronouns.

our	them	I	you	she	he
us	they	me	your	her	him
we	their	my	yours	hers	his
it	theirs	mine	ours	its	

1 Underline the pronouns in the following sentences.

   a. We all went to the movies to fill in time.

   b. Michelle and Sally thought he looked a little different today.

   c. I always enjoyed going shopping with my friend Katherine.

   d. Ms Donnell asked us to bring our permission slips back on Monday.

   e. Sticks and stones might break my bones but words will never hurt me.

2 Rewrite the sentences in the spaces provided, replacing the words or phrase in bold with the appropriate pronoun.

   a. **Dan and I** love to go hiking.

   _____

   b. They want **their son** to play cricket this year.

   _____

   c. **Geoff and Heidi** have moved to Waihi.

   _____

   d. **The teacher** called out to **George and Tama** to come to class.

   _____

   e. There was a time when the feelings between **Levi and me** were not good.

   _____

3

a. Read the following passage carefully. Underline the words you would replace with a pronoun.

Maree was determined that Maree would be the top of Maree's English class in the upcoming examination. Maree studied hard and asked Maree's teacher for extra work that Maree could do at home. Maree's mother was very impressed with the amount of work Maree was doing. Maree's mother decided that Maree's mother would help Maree and so Maree and Maree's mother did extra spelling and punctuation work also.

b. Now rewrite the passage including the pronouns you would use.

_____

_____

_____

_____

_____

_____

_____

_____

_____

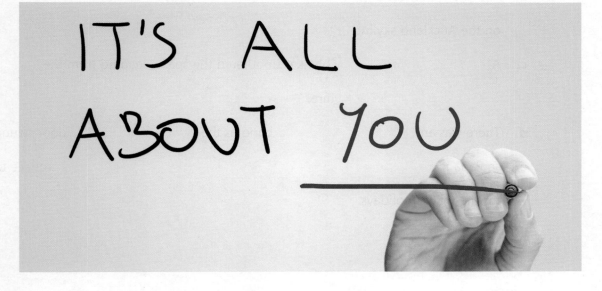

ADJECTIVES

Adjectives are 'describing' words.

Adjectives are the words we use to describe nouns. They help us add meaning to our chosen noun by describing the colour, size, shape, etc. For instance, the word 'car' is a noun.
But we, as writers, need to explain more about what the car is like.
To do this we use an adjective.

For example: *The **red** car.*

We can use more than one adjective to get across
our meaning. Remember to use a comma!

For example: *The **fast**, **red** car.*

1 **Underline the adjectives in the following sentences.**

a. The yellow clock ticked merrily.

b. Jonah picked up the ugly, black spider.

c. The book we had to read for English was huge!

d. The old man crossed the busy road at the pedestrian crossing.

e. Greer loved the look of the regular waves at Piha today. It was going to be awesome surf!

2 **Complete each sentence by choosing the appropriate adjective from the box below.**

fascinating	busy	dark	tall	blazing	pink
front	almighty	freezing	heavy	blue	straight

a. David quietly groped his way through the _____ room.

b. The Sky Tower stood _____ and _____

on the Auckland skyline.

c. A _____ blanket smothered the sparks leaping from the

_____ fire.

d. There was an _____ bang as the _____ door swung shut.

e. Te Papa is a _____ , _____ place to visit

for the school holidays.

ISBN: 9780170462983

3 Adjectives are exciting words to use but too often we are stuck in the same mode and refuse to try out new ones. A thesaurus is a brilliant resource to help us improve our vocabulary. Using a thesaurus, locate the following words and find two other words that could replace this word but improve the description. If you don't have access to a printed version then search for one on the Internet.

a. red

b. big

c. dark

d. wet

e. sharp

f. smelly

4 Replace the bold adjective in each sentence.

a. My dad is **great**. He loves to sail **tiny** yachts and enjoys working in our **big** garden but I really hate it when he wears his **floppy** sun hat and **floral** shirt!

b. I love our kapa haka group. We are **elegant** and **graceful**. I am like **beautiful** birds. My piupiu is made up of layers of **colourful** flax and my taniko is an **intricate** design. As we swing our poi and the boys leap in time to the **anicent** chants, my heart is filled with pride.

VERBS

A verb is a doing word.

The verb is the doing or action word in a sentence. For example:

The girl **ate** *her lunch.*

What did the girl do? She **ate** her lunch, so *ate* is the doing word, the verb.

1 **Underline the verbs in the following sentences.**

a. My mother sang a waiata.

b. I watched television.

c. The dog chased the cat.

d. I completed my homework.

e. The postie rode her bike.

2 **Write a verb in the spaces of the sentences below. For example: The All Black** *kicked* **the ball.**

a. The mouse _____ the bread.

b. Uncle Henry _____ his car.

c. I _____ my horse.

d. My dad _____ our dinner.

e. The aeroplane _____ through the clouds.

Verb tenses

The time of a verb is called the **tense**. The three tenses (or times) are:

present tense	the action is **happening now**
past tense	the action has **already happened**
future tense	the action **will happen**

ISBN: 9780170462983

3 Write down the verbs in the different tenses.

	past tense	present tense	future tense
sing	sang	sings/singing	will sing
a. jump			
b. write			
c. walk			
d. help			
e. finish			

Auxiliary verbs

There is a group of verbs that have a special job. They are called auxiliary verbs but it might help if you refer to them as 'helping verbs'. The word 'auxiliary' means a person or thing that supports or assists. How does the auxiliary verb help? Well, it helps, or supports, the main verb when we want to put it into different tenses.

For example: **Past**:   *I walked; I* **was** *walking or I* **have** *walked.*

            Present: *I walk; I* **am** *walking.*

            Future: *I* **will** *walk; I* **will be** *walking.*

Here is a list of the most common auxiliary verbs:

am	was	do	have	shall	could	must
is	were	does	has	will	should	might
are	be	did	had	can	would	may

4 Using the list above, put in the auxiliary verbs.
For example: **We** *are* **eating our lunch.**

a. When I _____ eaten my dinner, I _____ watch television.

b. They _____ asked to bring the pizzas.

c. If Mum _____ forgotten to any kai, I will go hungry.

d. I _____ buy my sister a gift tomorrow.

e. Where _____ my favourite top be?

ISBN: 9780170462983

MORE VERB PRACTICE

Let's put into practice what you know.

1 **Underline all the verbs (doing words) in the following sentences. For example: I *made* a cake.**

a. I do not know what to do.

b. My dog is so messy.

c. Baked beans are good for your heart.

d. I was watching television when you called.

e. I love playing computer games.

2 **Think about some of the things you do when you are at home, at school, when doing sport, or when you feel something. Write down some of these activities in the spaces provided below.**

At home, I like to ...
e.g. *sleep*

_____

_____

_____

_____

At school, I like to ...
e.g. *copy*

_____

_____

_____

_____

For sporting things, I like to ...
e.g. *swim*

_____

_____

_____

_____

Feelings I can experience are ...
e.g. *sadness*

_____

_____

_____

_____

ISBN: 9780170462983   PHOTOCOPYING OF THIS PAGE IS RESTRICTED UNDER LAW.

3 From the list below, put in an appropriate verb in each of the sentences.

cries	drinks	runs	throws	dives
looks	love	hate	frightened	watches
buys	steals	drive	vomits	snores
excites	stores	squashes	punctures	squeals

a. My uncle _____ to work.

b. My sister _____ in her sleep.

c. I _____ paua.

d. My children _____ me crazy.

e. The baby _____ all the time.

f. The deer _____ from the river.

g. The hunter _____ the deer.

h. The monster _____ the astronaut.

i. The boy _____ at the picture.

j. The ant _____ food for the winter.

4 Write some sentences of your own. Underline any verbs, including any auxiliary verbs. For example: I *will come* home soon.

a. _____

b. _____

c. _____

d. _____

e. _____

5 Change the following sentences into past tense by using auxiliary verbs. For example: I *eat*. (present tense) I *was eating*. (past tense)

a. I draw pictures. _____

b. I cook dinner. _____

c. She drives the car. _____

d. They play online games. _____

e. My friend rides his scooter. _____

ADVERBS

An adverb tells us how, when or where an action takes place.

Adverbs help us by giving extra meaning to verbs. They are sometimes hard to spot because they do several different jobs. They tell us:

HOW an action is done	*badly, well, lazily, quickly, fast, lovingly, keenly*
WHEN an action is done	*now, then, soon, before, after, since, yesterday, tomorrow*
WHERE an action is done	*anywhere, nowhere, everywhere, somewhere*

1 **The adverbs in the following sentences tell us how an action is done. Read the sentences carefully, underlining the adverbs.**

a. The telephone rang loudly.

b. The boy whispered softly to the girl.

c. Eating grapes quickly gives you a sore tummy.

d. I bumped my head hard on the desk.

e. The cat ran fast.

2 **The adverbs in the following sentences tell us when an action is done. Read the sentences carefully, underlining the adverbs.**

a. I want the dishes done now.

b. He has brushed his teeth since then.

c. Before we go to the movie, we need to go to the money machine.

d. I tried to call you yesterday but you weren't home.

e. My aunt goes home tomorrow.

3 **The adverbs in the following sentences tell us where an action is done. Read the sentences carefully, underlining the adverbs.**

a. I can't take you anywhere; you're too embarrassing.

b. If we go on holiday, the dog has nowhere to stay.

c. I haven't seen my bag anywhere.

d. We'll find somewhere to hang that painting.

e. He searched everywhere for his keys.

ISBN: 9780170462983

4 Write an appropriate adverb in the spaces provided.

a. I _____ rubbed out the phone number.

b. The teacher spoke _____ to the student.

c. The kura was closed _____ because of a water leak.

d. You need to write more _____ if you are to finish the exam.

e. My homework is _____ in my folder.

5 Rewrite the following paragraph, inserting interesting adverbs. Verbs that would suit having an adverb are printed in bold.

I **went** to town to **buy** some food. The shop was big and I **found** what I needed. On my list was breadcrumbs but I couldn't **find** them. I **asked** the shop assistant for some help. She **looked** at me and then **led** me back the way I had come. I **saw** the breadcrumbs, **took** them off the shelf, and **went** on my way. I **heard** the shop assistant **say** something under her breath.

_____

_____

_____

_____

_____

_____

_____

_____

_____

_____

CONJUNCTIONS

A conjunction is a word that joins words and sentences.

Co means together; **junction** is a place of joining, like the junction of a railway track. The purpose of a conjunction is to bring together words or sentences. Conjunctions give variety to your writing.

Sometimes the conjunction joins two sentences that could each make sense on its own. For example:

Zak got on his bike. He rode down the street.

Zak got on his bike and he rode down the street.

Sometimes the conjunction adds something to a sentence that would not make sense just on its own. For example:

Zak rode down the street. Around the corner.
(The second sentence doesn't make sense on its own.)

Zak rode down the street and around the corner.
(This makes sense.)

Below is a list of the most common conjunctions.

and	but	that	because	though	if
therefore	after	or/nor	when	before	unless
where	while	yet	for	than	how
whether	as	since	although	so	which

1 **Underline the conjunctions in the following sentences.**

a. The dog and the cat had a fight.

b. I went swimming because I was hot.

c. You can have some ice-cream but don't eat it all.

d. She's pretty good with the poi although not all the time.

e. You can go to Coronet Peak where they have a great ski field.

2 **Using the list of conjunctions above, replace the 'and' in each sentence with a more interesting conjunction.**

a. Josh was picked captain (and) _____ he is very popular.

b. We are planning a picnic (and) _____ it looks like rain.

c. The people stopped dancing (and) _____ the music was turned off.

ISBN: 9780170462983

d. I got a part in the chorus (and) _____ I wanted the lead in the play.

e. The Manu Kōrero speeches went overtime (and) _____ everyone arrived late to the wharekai.

3 Write out the following short sentences as **two** long ones by adding conjunctions.

> The meals arrived. Jeremy took the plates over to his father. He took a chair.
> He joined the table. He began to eat his dinner.

_____

_____

_____

_____

Sometimes a conjunction can be used at the beginning of a sentence as well as in the middle, for example:

They ate. Tom was silent.

While *they ate, Tom was silent.*

4 Complete the sentences by putting an appropriate conjunction in the spaces.

a. _____ Jack looked for Paul, the seat was empty.

b. _____ you went to bed late, you slept in.

c. _____ you like it or not, you can't afford it.

d. _____ you eat all your dinner, you can have some pudding.

e. _____ the sun came up, the birds began to sing.

5 Complete the sentences by putting an appropriate conjunction in the spaces.

a. I was overseas _____ you were born.

b. My grandmother trained as a teacher _____ she got married.

c. University costs a lot of money _____ I'm going to work for a while.

d. _____ I came from a large whānau, I sometimes felt lonely.

e. Time shall not weary them, _____ the years condemn them.

PREPOSITIONS

A preposition is a word that tells us the position
or place of something in relation to something else.
For example:

The cat sat *on* the dog.

Where did the cat sit?

On the dog.

A preposition is always followed by
a noun or pronoun.

Below is a list of the most common prepositions.

in	on	off	for	from	with
up	down	above	below	behind	before
after	over	under	into	out of	until
beneath	beyond	beside	around	against	along
across	among	between	through	near	inside

1 **Underline the** preposition **in each of the following sentences.**

   a. My dog went under the whare.

   b. The bird flew above the trees.

   c. My cellphone dropped down the toilet.

   d. A shark hunts beneath the sea.

   e. The book fell off the shelf.

2 **Using the list in the box above, put in the appropriate** preposition **.**

   a. I can swim _____ the water.

   b. My sister slides _____ the slide.

   c. My koro takes his glasses _____ him wherever he goes.

   d. My sister sat _____ the chair.

   e. He warned me not to go _____ the cave, but I didn't listen.

3 Using the list in the box on page 20, put in a different preposition. You can make some funny images with the preposition you choose.

a. The rubbish truck dumps the bins (beside) _____ the cars.

b. The learner driver went (around) _____ the cones on the road.

c. I went (through) _____ the woods.

d. The bird sat (on) _____ the bird bath.

e. I do my homework (before) _____ school.

4 Underline the prepositions in the following paragraph. There are four of them.

I had a problem with my garden. Everything grew too quickly in it and I never had the time to take out the weeds. Yesterday, I put concrete over it so now it will no longer be a problem.

5 Read the following passage and write down, in the space provided, each preposition you spot.

I stood on the diving board, nervous and excited, wondering if the butterflies in my stomach would settle. Above me, the loudspeaker crackled as the announcer told the audience sitting on the hill who I was. The flag master signalled me, and into the pool I went.

I was under the water for ages, bubbles swirling around me. Then I shot up and burst out into the air. My friend was to come after me so I swam beneath the diving tower, climbed up the ladder, and got out of the pool. My results flashed from the board – a perfect 10!

_____

_____

_____

_____

_____

_____

REVISION

Let's put into practice what you have learnt about parts of speech.

1 **Look carefully at the table below. The definitions and examples are jumbled up. Use the answer grid provided below to match the definitions and examples with their correct terms.**

Term	Definition	Example
1 Noun	a A describing word.	i The **audience** gave a standing ovation.
2 Proper noun	b Joins two sentences together.	ii We were crammed **in** the bus like sardines.
3 Abstract noun	c Describes the verb – i.e., it adds to the verb.	iii The **kettle** was on top of the **bench**.
4 Collective noun	d A doing word.	iv **red** car, **fast** car, **little** car, **old** car
5 Pronoun	e Nouns that refer to a specific person, place, etc. They must always have a capital letter.	v **She** raced down the stairs two at a time.
6 Adjective	f A word that tells us the position or place of something.	vi David **quietly** jumped the fence and crept to the window.
7 Verb	g A word that refers to a group or collection of similar people or things.	vii I have often suffered from **jealousy**.
8 Adverb	h A naming word.	viii He was **running** away from the dog. The dog **leapt** after him.
9 Conjunction	i Replaces the name of a person/noun.	ix On **Boxing Day** we relaxed in the sun.
10 Preposition	j Words that refer to qualities or things we cannot see.	x I walked down the road **and** caught the bus.

Answer grid

Term	1	2	3	4	5	6	7	8	9	10
Definition	h									
Example	iii									

ISBN: 9780170462983

2 **Identify the parts of speech in the following sentence.**

> I thought the arrival of the sparkling, new dishwasher would solve all my problems but it still needs someone to put in the dishes and take out the dishes.

a. Common noun

_____ _____ _____

_____ _____ _____

b. Pronoun

_____ _____ _____

c. Adjective

_____ _____

d. Verb

_____ _____ _____

_____ _____ _____

e. Preposition

_____ _____

f. Conjunction

_____ _____

3 **Identify the parts of speech in the following sentence.**

> We silently stood around the large hāngi then threw the sacks over its smoking embers.

a. Common noun

_____ _____ _____

b. Pronoun

_____ _____

c. Adjective

_____

d. Verb

_____

e. Adverb

_____

f. Preposition

_____

g. Conjunction

_____

CAPITAL LETTERS

Proper nouns must start with a capital letter.
Every new sentence must start with a capital letter.

Capital letters are used to:

- indicate proper nouns
- begin a sentence
- write the pronoun 'I'
- write the names of days and months
- write titles of books, plays, poems, films, ships, restaurants, etc.
- begin the first word inside quotation marks for direct speech.

1   **Rewrite the following, changing the lower case letters to capitals where necessary. For example:**

> the children go to glamorgan school.
> **T**he children go to **G**lamorgan **S**chool.

a.   my uncle is called charlie.

_____

b.   while watching television yesterday, mary fell asleep.

_____

c.   people call christchurch the garden city.

_____

d.   she would rather live in the country than the city.

_____

2   **This question focuses on the use of the capital letter 'I'. Rewrite the following, changing the lower case letters to capitals where necessary. For example:**

> i went for a swim yesterday. today i will read a book.
> **I** went for a swim yesterday. **T**oday **I** will read a book.

a.   my teacher's name is mrs milne and i enjoy her stories.

_____

ISBN: 9780170462983

b. my cat bonnie eats chef jellimeat. i think it smells terrible.

_____

c. i always have difficulty remembering to dot my 'i's.

_____

d. it's easy to see where to put a capital letter when it's not you writing the sentence.

_____

_____

3 This question focuses on using capitals for proper nouns. Rewrite the following, changing the lower case letters to capitals where necessary. For example:

> my father went north for waitangi day.
> **M**y father went north for **W**aitangi **D**ay.

a. it always rains on labour weekend.

_____

b. my brother sam is coming home in april.

_____

c. today is friday and tomorrow is saturday.

_____

d. the compass always points south when we head to gore.

_____

e. summer is my favourite season although i love skiing in winter.

_____

4 Now let's put all of the reasons for using a capital letter together. Rewrite the following, changing the lower case letters to capitals where necessary.

> during the easter holidays, my cousin came to take me to see a movie. i wanted
> to see the magic princess but he wanted to see blood bath four. we argued for
> ages then agreed that we would see my movie on tuesday and his on wednesday.

_____

_____

_____

_____

ISBN: 9780170462983

FULL STOPS

A full stop brings an end to a sentence.

The full stop is the most important punctuation mark of all. Without it, readers would not know where a sentence ends and another begins. Full stops help readers to understand the meaning of what they are reading.

1 **Using a red pen, put in the full stops and capital letters needed to make the sentences make sense.**

   a. my name is riley buchanan thomas

   b. i went down to the shops today to buy cadbury chocolate

   c. using computers is a wonderful way to present my assignments

   d. my favourite subject at school is māori

   e. on monday and friday I go to ballet practice

   f. i took three books out of the library this week

2 **Rewrite the following sentences, putting in the full stops and the capital letters. Be careful – they are a little bit harder than the earlier ones!**

   a. My daughter takes ages to go to bed she has a list of excuses to work through first

   _____

   _____

   b. She likes to read before she goes to sleep there is always a pile of books by her bed

   _____

   _____

   c. Tonight I saw a shooting star the sky was very black so it was easy to see the star

   _____

   _____

   d. Notice in newspaper: Tonight's lecture: our world ends at 9pm

   _____

   _____

   e. Dogs chase cats cats chase mice mice hide

   _____

   _____

3

a. Write out the following, putting in the full stops and capital letters where needed.

> The day began as normal my cat was curled up at the foot of my bed my dog was snoring loudly on the mat my mother shouted that it was time to get up I crawled out of bed and went to the shower then I got into my uniform and packed my school bag only when I went downstairs did I realise that it was saturday

_____

_____

_____

_____

_____

b. Write out the following, putting in the full stops and capital letters where needed.

> Summer is my favourite time of year I especially enjoy our family holidays at Mt Maunganui in January we drive down from Auckland and spend two weeks enjoying the sun, sand and surf we stay in the caravan park underneath the Mount I love hearing the waves as I drift off to sleep and being woken by the seagulls as they call the campers out of their beds

_____

_____

_____

_____

_____

COMMAS

The comma tells the reader when to take a short pause in a sentence, or when a word or words need to be separated within a sentence.

The comma tells the reader when to take a breath while reading a sentence aloud. There are three main ways a comma is used:

1. To divide a sentence into parts, making the ideas easier to read and understand.
   For example:

Without the comma	*Can we go see the tigers eat Mum?*
With the comma	*Can we go see the tigers eat, Mum?*

   Where you place the comma is important because it can change the meaning of your sentence.
   For example:

   With the comma in one place.
   I told you, today you must clean your room.

   With the comma in another place.
   I told you today, you must clean your room.

2. To separate items in a list. For example:

   I had to buy milk, spaghetti, mushrooms, meat and marshmallows at the supermarket today.

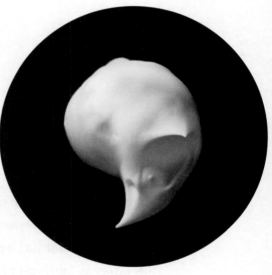

3. To separate an explanation within a sentence.
   For example:

   Russell, who is my husband, will be here at eleven.

Clue: If you find it difficult to place commas in a sentence, remember that where you take a breath should have a punctuation mark.

 Using a red pen, put in the commas so the sentences make sense:

a. The lady put her seat belt on a little bit annoyed with her son.

b. The children sat down in their chairs silently watching their teacher.

c. Quickly take the plate from that tamaiti.

d. He rolled on to the mat his legs tucked under him and his hands stretched out.

e. If you can't stop complaining go to your room.

ISBN: 9780170462983

2 Using a red pen, put in the commas where they are needed to separate the lists.

a. I like onions garlic gherkins and pickles but not olives.

b. She invited her neighbour her teacher and her coach to the prize giving.

c. John came first Sam second Daniel third and I came last.

d. How do you start a flea race? One two flea go!

e. We were responsible for the pōwhiri: Te Atakura did the karanga Tawhiri started the haka Matua Hēmi led the karakia and I made the tea.

3 Using a red pen, put in the commas where they are needed to separate the explanations.

a. Ms Howell the teacher with the curly hair is the person taking names.

b. Ani had crossed the road thank goodness before the accident took place.

c. Mrs Raven the school guidance counsellor has an appointment with my parents at 12 o'clock.

d. Snakes and spiders which I hate are commonly found in the Australian outback.

e. *The Lord of the Rings* my favourite book has been made into a movie.

4 Using a red pen, put in the commas where they are needed in the following passage.

Eru and Rikki twin brothers wanted their grandmother to make them pikelets. In order for her to be able to complete the recipe she asked the boys to go and get some things from the supermarket. They had to get eggs butter and flour but they came home with eggs sugar and milk! Gran who was a cheerful lady couldn't believe her eyes as she went through the plastic bag. Eru and Rikki were sent to try again. Hopefully they will do better this time.

APOSTROPHES

The apostrophe has two main purposes:

1. To show ownership.
2. To show where one or more letters is missed out in a contraction (making two words into one).

To show ownership

Ask yourself: 'who is the owner?' Then put the apostrophe after the last letter of the owner's name.

If the word does not end in s, add an apostrophe + s = 's.
*The **man's** tie was crooked.* (man + 's = man's)

If the word does end in s, add an apostrophe after the s.
*Our three **cats'** bowls were full.* (cats + ' = cats')

1 Ask yourself 'who is the owner?' Then using a red pen, write in the apostrophe and 's'.

a. My mother necklace is broken.

b. The car door is crushed.

c. This is my brother son.

d. Our form roll book was lost.

e. The teacher nose dribbled.

2 Using a red pen, write in the apostrophe.

a. My two brothers children are older than mine.

b. Your parents car is cool.

c. The old folks home is a nice place.

d. The ladies meals were cold.

e. The high school teams coaches are very capable.

ISBN: 9780170462983

3 **Rewrite the following phrases using an apostrophe to show ownership.**
For example: *the bike belonging to the boy*: *the boy's bike*

   a. the page of the book _____

   b. the baby of the mother _____

   c. the driver of the car _____

   d. the books of the students _____

   e. the wages of the workers _____

The shortening apostrophe

When you join two words and leave out one or more letters, you use an apostrophe to show that you have done this.

   I am going to the movies.

   I'm going to the movies. (**I** and **am** are joined to form **I'm**)

4 **Write out the following, using the apostrophe to shorten the words.**
For example: *did not = didn't*

   a. you are _____

   b. can not _____

   c. we will _____

   d. you have _____

   e. should not _____

5 **Rewrite in full the following contractions.**
For example: *aren't = are not*

   a. it's _____

   b. couldn't _____

   c. should've _____

   d. you'll _____

   e. that's _____

MORE APOSTROPHES

Let's put into practice what you know.

1 **Using a red pen, write in the apostrophe.**

   a. Her brothers skateboard was stolen.

   b. I ate my sisters ice-cream.

   c. The farmers gumboots were dirty.

   d. My chairs broken.

   e. Your beds cool.

2 **Using a red pen, write in the apostrophes.**

   a. My mothers temper is worse than my fathers.

   b. The computers hard drive wont work.

   c. This is my brothers sister-in-laws mother.

   d. The planes flight paths were mixed up.

   e. His childrens school is closer than ours.

3 **Write out the following, using the apostrophe to shorten the words.**

   a. I am   _____

   b. he is   _____

   c. they are   _____

   d. I will not   _____

   e. they have   _____

4 **Rewrite in full the following contractions.**

   a. there's   _____

   b. I'll   _____

   c. I'd   _____

   d. they'd   _____

   e. she'd   _____

ISBN: 9780170462983

Special ownership words

There are special words that also show ownership but do not need to use an apostrophe. They are words that mean ownership. Below is a list of commonly used ownership words.

mine	your	yours	their	theirs
ours	its	his	hers	our

5 **Using the list above, fill in the spaces below to complete the sentences.**

a. Those pencils are _____. Give them to me.

b. I wish they would wash _____ feet before they came inside.

c. That man is driving with _____ eyes closed.

d. _____ house is better than _____.

e. She wishes _____ was as good as _____.

6 **Using the list in the box above, write out your own short sentences that include possessive pronouns.**

a. _____

b. _____

c. _____

d. _____

e. _____

7 **Using a red pen, correct the following sentences. Read them carefully first!**

a. I dont like it when my sisters boyfriend teases me.

b. Your supposed to give me your ticket before you go in.

c. My uncles aunt cant wait until we take her to the speedway.

d. Flyings okay so long as youve got you're motion sickness pills.

   And a final extra tricky one . . .

e. There taking there picnic over there, away from our's.

SPEECH MARKS

Speech marks are used to show the words being said by a speaker.

Only the actual words spoken go inside the speech marks but the punctuation of the whole sentence can seem a little confusing. Here is how it goes.

There are three ways in which speech marks can be applied:

1. For spoken words at the beginning of the sentence:
    For example: *'**Two tickets to Wellington**,' he said.*

2. For spoken words at the end of the sentence:
    For example: *He said,* *'**Two tickets to Wellington**.'*

3. For spoken words in the middle of the sentence:
    For example: *'**Two tickets**,' he said,* *'**to Wellington**.'*

Where to place the comma, the full stop and other things:

All commas, full stops, question marks and exclamation marks that are part of the spoken sentence stay inside the speech marks. When the sentence is 'interrupted', use a comma if the sentence continues as in the third example above. Otherwise use a full stop at the end of the description of who is speaking. For example:

> *'**I am happy at home**,' she remarked.*
> *'**It's the quietest place to be**.'*

Where to place the capital letters:

> *'**Two tickets to Wellington**,' he said.*

Try to imagine the whole sentence without the add-ons or interruptions. Ask yourself: where would I normally put the capitals? The beginning of the spoken sentence above is 'Two' and, as it is the beginning, it starts with a capital letter. In the third example at the top, the word 'to' does not have a capital letter because it is in the middle section of the sentence.

ISBN: 9780170462983   PHOTOCOPYING OF THIS PAGE IS RESTRICTED UNDER LAW.

ANSWERS

(This four-page section can be removed from the centre of the book.)

PRE-TEST *pages 2–3*

1 a man c car
   b cat d Love
2 a We c You
   b I d It
3 a smelly c loud
   b cold d disgusting
4 a sings c finished
   b chased d rode
5 a was c is
   b can d should
6 a fast c yesterday
   b badly d anywhere
7 a and c but
   b because d although
8 a under c down
   b above d beneath
9 a My, Aroha
   b While, Molly
   c People, Auckland, (The) City, Sails
   d It
10 a Monday's c can't
   b girls' d They're
11 a Before you go to bed, brush your teeth.
   b Can we go see the tigers eat, Mum?
   c If you love something, set it free.
   d If it was yours, it will return to you.
12 a 'What are you doing?' demanded the policeman.
   b 'Nothing,' replied the boy. 'I'm just looking.'
   c The policeman glared. 'Are you being cheeky?'
   d 'No, sir.'

PARTS OF SPEECH

Common nouns *page 4*

1 a dog, tail
   b sailor, rope, people, boat
   c cake, oven
   d student, encyclopaedia, shelf, research
   e mountain, people, lookout
2 Shannon/Ashley, Ashley/Shannon, track, beach, shed, creek, Shannon/Ashley, towel, rays, Ashley/Shannon, jandals, water.
3 Guardian/parent/teacher to check.

Proper nouns *page 5*

1 a Mr Cottle, Christchurch, Oamaru
   b Jason, Patrick, Avondale College
   c Wednesday, Karen
   d Connor, New Zealand, Ireland
   e Waverley, Te Papa, Wellington
2 a Tāupo, September
   b Waikato River
   c Dr McBride, Starship Children's Hospital, Monday
   d Dame Te Atairangikaahu, Māori, Tuheitia Paki
   e Good Friday, Easter, Sunday

Collective nouns *page 6*

1 a crew b school
   c government d team
   e committee
2 a army b colony
   c bouquet d gang
   e pride f cluster
   g fleet h litter
   i choir j gaggle

Abstract nouns *page 7*

1 a jealousy d peace
   b quietness e honesty
   c loyalty
2 a loneliness c uselessness
   b happiness d hopelessness
3 a friendship c leadership
   b ownership d scholarship
4 a sisterhood c knighthood
   b neighbourhood d childhood

Pronouns *pages 8–9*

1 a We b he
   c I, my d us, our
   e my, me
2 a We love to go hiking.
   b They want him to play cricket this year.
   c They have moved to Waihi.
   d He/She called out to them to come to class.
   e There was a time when the feelings between us were not good.
3 b Maree was determined that she would be the top of her English class in the upcoming examination. She studied hard and asked her teacher for extra work that she could do at home. Maree's mother was very impressed with the amount of work she was doing. She decided that she would help her and so Maree and her mother did extra spelling and punctuation work also.

Adjectives *pages 10–11*

1 a yellow b ugly, black
   c huge
   d old, busy, pedestrian
   e regular, awesome
2 a dark b straight, tall
   c heavy, blazing d almighty, front
   e fascinating, busy
3 Guardian/parent/teacher to check.
4 Guardian/parent/teacher to check.

Verbs *pages 12–13*

1 a sang b watched
   c chased d completed
   e rode
2 Guardian/parent/teacher to check.
3 a jumped, jumps, will jump
   b wrote, writes, will write
   c walked, walks, will walk
   d helped, helps, will help
   e finished, finishes, will finish
4 a have, will b were
   c has
   d shall/will/can/could/should/must/might/may
   e could/can/might/would

More verb practice *pages 14–15*

1 a do, know, do b is
   c are
   d was watching, called
   e love playing
2 Guardian/parent/teacher to check.
3 *Our choices:*
   a runs b snores
   c love d drive
   e cries f drinks

g watches h frightened
i looks j stores
4 Guardian/parent/teacher to check.
5 a I was drawing pictures.
   b I was cooking dinner.
   c She was driving the car.
   d They were playing online games.
   e My friend was riding his scooter.

Adverbs *pages 16–17*

1 a loudly b softly
   c quickly d hard
   e fast
2 a now b since (then)
   c Before d yesterday
   e tomorrow
3 a anywhere b nowhere
   c anywhere d somewhere
   e everywhere
4 *Our choices:*
   a quickly b severely
   c yesterday d efficiently
   e somewhere
5 Guardian/parent/teacher to check.

Conjunctions *pages 18–19*

1 a and b because
   c but d although
   e where
2 *Our choices:*
   a because b although
   c after d but
   e therefore/so
3 *Our choices:*
   The meals arrived and Jeremy took the plates over to his father. Then he took a chair and joined the table before he began to eat his dinner.
4 *Our choices:*
   a When b Because
   c Whether d If
   e When
5 *Our choices:*
   a when b before
   c so d Because/Although
   e nor

Prepositions *pages 20–21*

1 a under b above
   c down d beneath
   e off
2 a under b down
   c with d on
   e into
3 Guardian/parent/teacher to check.
4 with, in, out, over
5 on, in, Above, on, into, under, around, up, out, into, after, beneath, up, out of, from

Revision *pages 22–23*

1

Term	1	2	3	4	5	6	7	8	9	10
Definition	h	e	j	g	i	a	d	c	b	f
Example	iii	ix	vii	i	v	iv	viii	vi	x	ii

2 a arrival, dishwasher, problems, someone, dishes, dishes
   b I, my, it c sparkling, new, all
   d thought, would, solve, needs, put, take
   e of, in, out f but, and
3 a hāngi, sacks, embers
   b We, its c large
   d stood e silently
   f around, over g then

PUNCTUATION, SPELLING AND GRAMMAR

Capital letters *pages 24–25*

1 a My uncle is called Charlie.
  b While watching television yesterday, Mary fell asleep.
  c People call Christchurch The/the Garden City.
  d She would rather live in the country than the city.

2 a My teacher's name is Mrs Milne and I enjoy her stories.
  b My cat Bonnie eats Chef Jellimeat. I think it smells terrible.
  c I always have difficulty remembering to dot my 'i's.
  d It's easy to see where to put a capital letter when it's not you writing the sentence.

3 a It always rains on Labour Weekend.
  b My brother Sam is coming home in April.
  c Today is Friday and tomorrow is Saturday.
  d The compass always points south when we head to Gore.
  e Summer is my favourite season although I love skiing in winter.

4 During the Easter holidays, my cousin came to take me to see a movie. I wanted to see *The Magic Princess* but he wanted to see *Blood Bath Four*. We argued for ages then agreed that we would see my movie on Tuesday and his on Wednesday.

Full stops *pages 26–27*

1 a My name is Riley Buchanan Thomas.
  b I went down to the shops today to buy Cadbury chocolate.
  c Using computers is a wonderful way to present my assignments.
  d My favourite subject at school is Māori.
  e On Monday and Friday I go to ballet practice.
  f I took three books out of the library this week.

2 a My daughter takes ages to go to bed. She has a list of excuses to work through first.
  b She likes to read before she goes to sleep. There is always a pile of books by her bed.
  c Tonight I saw a shooting star. The sky was very black so it was easy to see the star.
  d Notice in newspaper: Tonight's lecture: Our world. Ends at 9pm.
  e Dogs chase cats. Cats chase mice. Mice hide.

3 a The day began as normal. My cat was curled up at the foot of my bed. My dog was snoring loudly on the mat. My mother shouted that it was time to get up. I crawled out of bed and went to the shower. Then I got into my uniform and packed my school bag. Only when I went downstairs did I realise that it was Saturday.

3 b Summer is my favourite time of year. I especially enjoy our family holidays at Mt Maunganui in January. We drive down from Auckland and spend two weeks enjoying the sun, sand and surf. We stay in the caravan park underneath the Mount. I love hearing the waves as I drift off to sleep and being woken by the seagulls as they call the campers out of their beds.

Commas *pages 28–29*

1 a The lady put her seat belt on, a little bit annoyed with her son.
  b The children sat down in their chairs silently, watching their teacher. or The children sat down in their chairs, silently watching their teacher.
  c Quickly, take the plate from that tamaiti.
  d He rolled on to the mat, his legs tucked under him and his hands stretched out.
  e If you can't stop complaining, go to your room.

2 a I like onions, garlic, gherkins and pickles, but not olives.
  b She invited her neighbour, her teacher, and her coach to the prize giving.
  c John came first, Sam second, Daniel third, and I came last.
  d How do you start a flea race? One, two, flea, go!
  e We were responsible for the pōwhiri: Te Atakura did the karanga, Tawhiri started the haka, Matua Hēmi led the karakia and I made the tea.

3 a Ms Howell, the teacher with the curly hair, is the person taking names.
  b Ani had crossed the road, thank goodness, before the accident took place.
  c Mrs Raven, the school guidance counsellor, has an appointment with my parents at 12 o'clock.
  d Snakes and spiders, which I hate, are commonly found in the Australian outback.
  e *The Lord of the Rings*, my favourite book, has been made into a movie.

4 Eru and Rikki, twin brothers, wanted their grandmother to make them pikelets. In order for her to be able to complete the recipe, she asked the boys to go and get some things from the supermarket. They had to get eggs, butter and flour, but they came home with eggs, sugar and milk! Gran, who was a cheerful lady, couldn't believe her eyes as she went through the plastic bag. Eru and Rikki were sent to try again. Hopefully, they will do better this time.

Apostrophes *pages 30–31*

1 a My mother's necklace is broken.
  b The car's door is crushed.
  c This is my brother's son.
  d Our form's roll book was lost.
  e The teacher's nose dribbled.

2 a My two brothers' children are older than mine.
  b Your parents' car is cool.
  c The old folks' home is a nice place.
  d The ladies' meals were cold.
  e The high school teams' coaches are very capable.

3 a The book's page.
  b The mother's baby.
  c The car's driver.

d The students' books.
  e The workers' wages.

4 a you're   b can't
  c we'll   d you've
  e shouldn't

5 a it is/has   b could not
  c should have d you will
  e that is/has

More apostrophes *pages 32–33*

1 a Her brother's skateboard was stolen.
  b I ate my sister's ice-cream.
  c The farmer's gumboots were dirty.
  d My chair's broken.
  e Your bed's cool.

2 a My mother's temper is worse than my father's.
  b The computer's hard drive won't work.
  c This is my brother's sister-in-law's mother.
  d The planes' flight paths were mixed up.
  e His children's school is closer than ours.

3 a I'm   b he's
  c they're   d I won't/I'll not
  e they've

4 a there is/has   b I will/shall
  c I would/had   d they would/had
  e she would/had

5 *Our choices:*
  a mine   b their
  c his   d Their, ours
  e hers, yours

6 Guardian/parent/teacher to check.

7 a I don't like it when my sister's boyfriend teases me.
  b You're supposed to give me your ticket before you go in.
  c My uncle's aunt can't wait until we take her to the speedway.
  d Flying's okay so long as you've got your motion sickness pills.
  e They're taking their picnic over there, away from ours.

Speech marks *pages 34–35*

1 a 'You always boss me around, even when I'm not home,' she shouted.
  b She shouted, 'You always boss me around, even when I'm not home.'
  c 'You always boss me around,' she shouted, 'even when I'm not home.'

2 a 'Mrs Harvey, are you okay?'
    'I feel very tired.' She closed her eyes. 'I think I'll have a little sleep.'
    'I'm not sure that's such a good idea,' Sophie said quickly. 'How 'bout I turn on the radio?'
  b 'How old are you?' Malcolm asked.
    'How old are you?' Sophie replied.
    'Almost eleven.'
    'Kinda young to be out here on your own.'
    'No. I've done it for ages.' Malcolm turned to her and smiled. 'I've got secret spots.'

Simple sentences *pages 36–37*

1 a subject, verb, object
  b subject, verb, object
  c subject, verb, object
  d subject, verb, object
  e subject, verb, object

2 Guardian/parent/teacher to check.

3 Then she changed her clothes.

4-5 Guardian/parent/teacher to check.

Compound sentences
pages 38–39

1 **a** (The little girl put on a dress) and (she put on her shoes).
   b (Will you take the bus) or (do you want me to take you?)
   c (The cat meowed all night) so (everyone slept badly).
   d (Dinosaurs are extinct) but (they are still popular).
   e (I am tired); (I didn't get much sleep last night).

2 **a** He entered the room but he did not sit down.
   b The dog is large but he is kind.
   c Mum is patient so she never gets angry.
   d I came home late so I am in trouble.
   e The gauge says empty so we need to get petrol.

3 It didn't bother her much but she got sick of the teasing at school.

4 Guardian/parent/teacher to check.

5 Guardian/parent/teacher to check.

Spelling trouble-shooting
pages 40–41

1 **a** there   **b** their
   c they're   **d** their
   e There, they're

2 **a** effects   **b** effect
   c affects   **d** effect
   e affect   **f** effect, affected

3 **a** accept   **b** except
   c accept   **d** accept, except
   e accept, except

4 **a** You're   **b** your
   c your   **d** You're
   e Your

5 **a** weather   **b** whether
   c weather   **d** weather

Revision and practice
pages 42–43

1 Megan appeared carrying a greasy bag in one hand. 'Time for breakfast,' she said, as she plonked herself down beside him. 'I thought you might be hungry.'

   'I am,' Jeremy answered. 'How much?'

   'Nuffin,' Megan said through a mouth filled with mince pie. 'I borrowed it.'

   'You stole it? Man, you're quick.' He pulled his pie out of the bag.

   'It's not stealing in the literal sense of the word. It's not like we'll be taking anything off the ship.'

   'What are you on about?'

   'We're gonna be here for a few hours. By that time this stuff would have gone through our digestive systems . . .'

   'You are so disgusting!'

   'Seriously, we don't leave the boat with anything more than we came on.'

POETIC TECHNIQUES

Similes *pages 44–45*

1 **a** Yes   **b** Yes
   c No   **d** Yes
   e No

2 smile was as wide as the sea
   piled like a pyramid
   as blue as the sky
   sounded like a happy angel

3 **a** red   **b** straight
   c brave   **d** quiet
   e smooth   **f** sharp
   g slow   **h** blue
   i flat   **j** fit
   k stubborn   **l** quick

4 **a** strong/ox   **b** slow/snail
   c red/ruby   **d** pink/candy floss
   e hard/concrete   **f** round/moon

Metaphors *pages 46–47*

1 **a** Yes   **b** No
   c Yes   **d** Yes
   e No

2 soaking up the sun, was a row of soldiers, brightly coloured people enjoying the ride

3 *Suggestions only:*
   a The boat was an island in the rolling sea.
   b From the helicopter the fields were a patchwork quilt.
   c My watch strap was a snake wrapped firmly around my wrist.
   d Her eyes were blazing pools of fire.
   e The grapefruit is the sun of the citrus fruit.

4 Guardian/parent/teacher to check.

Personification *pages 48–49*

1 **a** Yes   **b** No
   c No   **d** Yes
   e No

2 **a** bbq tongs/jaws
   b mailbox/mouth
   c leaves/danced
   d bananas/sleeping
   e zip/teeth

3 streetlights winked
   storm threatened
   life source
   wind tearing
   pulling at her jacket
   torch danced
   searching erratically
   light called out to her

4 **a** chattered   **b** danced
   c grabbed
   d insisted on creeping
   e roared, standing guard

5 Guardian/parent/teacher to check.

Alliteration *pages 50–51*

1 **a** t   **b** h
   c s   **d** f
   e p   **f** w

2 **a** blue, bike
   b *Street*, starts, seven
   c Serious, silently, swimming
   d knitted, never-ending, nimble, knitting, needles
   e cautious, climbed, cabbage

3 *Suggestions only:*
   a Our boat sailed swiftly out to sea.
   b The dolphins darted daintily past the deck.
   c The fly flew frequently around my head.
   d Paul sent a postcard from Puerto Rico where he had sunbathed, surfed and swum all week.

4 Guardian/parent/teacher to check.

Onomatopoeia *pages 52–53*

1 **a** tick, tick, tick   **b** boom
   c yapped   **d** chirped
   e Woosh   **f** fizzed

2 **a** bang   **b** sizzle
   c slop   **d** thud
   e tapped   **f** ouch

3 crashed, squelched, oozed, drip (x3), cracked, screeched, twanged, pinged

4 *Suggestions only:*
   a thwack/thud
   b purr/meow
   c splash/smack/slap
   d squelch/slop/squish/slush
   e rumble
   f slurp
   g smash
   h cock-a-doodle-doo

5 Guardian/parent/teacher to check.

Assonance *page 54*

1 **a** Rebecca sleeps neatly in the bed.
   b boat, soaked
   c like, ice
   d ape, ate
   e through, blue

2 **a** fire, shyly
   b cheated, beep
   c two, shoes
   d Stuart, knew, to, do
   e were, further
       than, that

Rhyme *page 55*

1 spent/bent, dog/bog, hose/pose, coat/boat, man/can, Ben/pen, cask/mask

2 **a** nice/ice, kind/mind
   b sun/fun, sail/tail
   c school/pool, well/swell

3 Guardian/parent/teacher to check.

Revision *pages 56–57*

1 The sun, like the colour of summer corn … and, like ants, File singly back to the car.

2 While the beach is a patchwork quilt Its thick umbrella of leaves.

3 *Choose from:*
   The sun … Spreads its arms wide to give us warmth.
   … the lapping of waves, their fingers Trying to catch hold of our feet.
   … the sun bows farewell

4 *Choose from:*
   doors slam and children cheer
   Suntan lotion is slopped and slapped
   shirts slip off and togs slip up
   bright beach balls
   gulls screech their goodbyes.

5 *Choose from:* slam, slopped, slapped, whooping, lapping, screech

6 *Choose from:* us shade under, bows farewell

EXTRA PRACTICE 1
pages 58–59

1 **a** beach, things, liners, ships, current, stuff, pōhutukawa, place, pool, glasses, tide, mark, water
   b Robbie, Grandad, Frisbee
   c We, me, his, it, I, her
   d excellent, cruise, just right, interesting, south, twisted, best, settling, munted, high
   e beachcombing, said, pass (by), finding, washed, pass, bring, started, found, kept, swept, found
   f were, was, We'd
   g slowly

h because, and, but

i (pass) by, in, down, near, every now and then, along

2 'Well?' he asked, pulling the hood of his cloak tightly over his nose to avoid being overwhelmed by the stench from the cauldron and the moist hot air of the dirty hut.

3 **1** compound
  2 simple
  3 simple
  4 compound
  5 simple

4 **a** It's, weather
  b there
  c affects
  d except
  e You're, your
  f Whether
  g accept
  h They're
  i affected
  j Their

EXTRA PRACTICE 2
pages 60–61

1 **a** rain, windscreen, streetlights, glow, nail, wipers, action, curve
  b Emma
  c her, she
  d heavy (shower), blackened, eerie, incandescent, glossy, red
  e splattered, blurring, creating, flicked, spun, whirring, skidded
  f quickly
  g and
  h against, into, around

2 As one the three strange women turned from the blackened pot cooking over a fire. Each of them held a wooden cup. The eldest of the three stepped forward, the flickering light from the fire deepening the craggy lines in her face, and lifted her cup to him. 'Speak,' she demanded.

3 It's not fair! You're always on Mum's computer. I'm supposed to finish my maths homework by tonight and it's on her hard drive. You should've asked first. Why don't you go to Matt's house and play your games on his computer?

4 **a** there
  b effects
  c accept
  d your
  e weather
  f except
  g their
  h effect
  i whether
  j They're

EXTRA PRACTICE 3
pages 62–63

1 **a** lump, rocks, body, stomach, beach, adult, looks, brother, son, years, inches
  b Robbie, I, Grandad
  c mood, sissy, (his) way,
  d My, I, We, him, me, his, he
  e fleshy, dead, rotting, best, little, tough, first born, stronger, tougher, younger, shorter

f asked, pointing, huddled, looks, squeezed, find, go, told, Don't, said, giving, knew, reminding,

g What (is), wasn't, should, have, can be

h really, sometimes

i and, though, even

2 The wipers swished sluggishly backwards and forwards across the windscreen. It was cold and the wet weather that had nagged at them all the way from Auckland started to irritate. Even Sophie's borrowed army-issue overcoat could not keep her warm. She was miserable.

3 **a** Personification
  b Simile
  c Metaphor
  d Personification
  e Metaphor
  f Personification/Simile
  g Personification
  h Simile

4 **a** creek
  b through
  c principal
  d pale
  e waste
  f sent
  g Your, you're
  h bare
  i scene
  j pane

EXTRA PRACTICE 4
pages 64–65

1 **a** car, headlights, nothing, rain, bank, fall, seats
  b Sophie
  c their, them, someone's
  d sleeting, hard
  e lurched, watched, pointing, tumbled, pushed, screaming
  f violently, horror
  g and, but, as
  h in, into, over, against

2 I've never liked swimming. I just can't seem to relax in the water. It's as if I'm always fighting to get my breath and I just never learnt how to dive. It's pretty hard to look cool if you have to lower yourself carefully down the side of the pool while everyone else is doing Olympic-style dives; their bodies breaking the surface of the water like arrows.

3 **a** 'I guess it's a very individual thing,' she says. 'When you see someone wearing a tā moko you wonder if that's what represents them. Does it say something important about who they are?'
  b 'But I don't want to go home yet.' wailed Anna to her aunt.
'I know Anna but this is the easiest way for everyone.'
  c 'Would you like cracked pepper with your soup?' the waiter asked.
  d The tourist stood in the Octagon. 'Excuse me?' he asked a couple of kids with skateboards. 'Can you point me in the direction of the railway station?'
  e 'My favourite foods are bananas, apples and peaches,' she told the interviewer. 'But I'm also partial to a nice piece of chocolate cake.'

4 **a** weather
  b They're
  c affect
  d except
  e You're, your
  f Whether
  g accept
  h there
  i effect
  j their

FINAL TEST *pages 66–68*

1 **a** *One of:* men, hill
  b General Blake
  c *One of:* squad, army
  d disobedient
  e they
  f young
  g *One of:* made, stand, were being, ran, sit
  h quickly
  i However, and
  j on

2 **a** *One of:* men, sheep, pen, marshmallows, milk
  b Pascall
  c flock
  d *One of:* they, them
  e square
  f realised, get, tempt
  g before (long), would have
  h sneakily
  i and
  j *One of:* in, with

3 **a** My name is Seung and I live in Auckland. I like apples, pears, bananas and grapes.
  b I crashed my father's car because I was watching the dog trip over its lead.
  c Your house is in Wellington. Ours is in Christchurch where birds fly north for the winter and where Dad says you can't go to the beach.
  d The boy's pencil case was left there with his friends' bags and their pencil cases.
  e 'Usually in the evening when the sky is red,' he explained, 'the following day is fine. But,' he went on, 'that's not what we'll rely on. I'll go ring the Met Service.' That's my grandfather Ted. He's the practical sort.

4 **a** *Two of:* You must answer all the questions.
It's that simple.
Try not to look at the answers.
  b This test is a difficult one but you can do it if you go carefully.
Read over all that you have done and check your work is correct.

5 **a** like unruly children
  b It had been sheer heaven.
  c *One of:* The heat … reluctant to let go of its grasp
the bach sat silent, dark, waiting
  d *One of:* hung heavily; sat silent; dusty dunes; bodies, backs burnt and bruised
  e *One of:* up … dusty; now with the sound
  f *One of:* booming, jangling

1 **Punctuate the following with speech marks, commas and full stops in the style described on the previous page to make the meaning clear.**

a. You always boss me around even when I'm not home she shouted

_____

_____

b. She shouted You always boss me around even when I'm not home

_____

_____

c. You always boss me around she shouted even when I'm not home

_____

_____

2 **Write out the following, putting in all the speech marks to make the sense clear.**

a. Mrs Harvey are you okay? I feel very tired. She closed her eyes. I think I'll have a little sleep. I'm not sure that's such a good idea, Sophie said quickly. How 'bout I turn on the radio?

_____

_____

_____

_____

b. How old are you? Malcolm asked. How old are you? Sophie replied. Almost eleven. Kinda young to be out here on your own. No. I've done it for ages.
Malcolm turned to her and smiled. I've got secret spots.

_____

_____

_____

_____

SIMPLE SENTENCES

A simple sentence is a group of words that includes a verb and which makes sense on its own.

A simple sentence needs only:
   one verb,
   one thing to do the action (called the subject), and
   something to react against it (the object),

although you don't always need the object for the sentence to make sense.

For example: *The girl* (subject) *drew* (verb) *the picture* (object).
               The girl (subject) *drew* (verb).

These two examples are simple sentences because each has a verb and a subject and makes sense on its own.

To begin every simple sentence with the subject first would be boring.
You can change the order around to create a special effect. For example:

   A raindrop sparkled in the sun.
   In the sun, a raindrop sparkled.
   Sparkling in the sun was a raindrop.

We can imagine that a simple sentence is like a train engine. An engine doesn't need anything else to help it move along the tracks. It can go around quite happily on its own. It is the same with a simple sentence: it doesn't need any extra words or phrases to help it make sense.

1   **In the space provided, write down subject, verb, object as is appropriate.**
        Ask yourself: What is the action? Who is doing it?
        For example: The man (subject) rowed (verb) the boat (object).

a.   My sister _____ pulled out _____ all her clothes _____ .

b.   The dog _____ bit _____ the man _____ .

c.   I _____ wrote _____ a letter _____ .

d.   My mother _____ talks _____ to me _____ .

e.   We _____ watched _____ the cricket _____ .

ISBN: 9780170462983

2 In the spaces below, write down words that make up a **simple sentence**. For example: **(Subject)** *My horse* **(verb)** *eats* **(object)** *the grass*.

a. (Subject) _____ (verb) _____ (object) _____

b. (Subject) _____ (verb) _____ (object) _____

c. (Subject) _____ (verb) _____ (object) _____

d. (Subject) _____ (verb) _____ (object) _____

e. (Subject) _____ (verb) _____ (object) _____

3 Underline the **simple sentence** from the following paragraph.

Waiting for the sun to go down, Asha set about tidying her room and setting up the barbecue area before people began to arrive. Then she changed her clothes. Soon the backyard was filled with the sounds of laughter and little children squealing as they played chase through their parents' legs.

4 Write some of your own examples of simple sentences.

a. _____

b. _____

c. _____

d. _____

e. _____

5 For each sentence in question 4, identify the **subject**, the **verb** and the **object** (if applicable).

a. (Subject) _____ (verb) _____ (object) _____

b. (Subject) _____ (verb) _____ (object) _____

c. (Subject) _____ (verb) _____ (object) _____

d. (Subject) _____ (verb) _____ (object) _____

e. (Subject) _____ (verb) _____ (object) _____

COMPOUND SENTENCES

A compound sentence is two or more simple sentences joined together with a conjunction (a joining word) or separated by a semi-colon.

If we wrote in simple sentences all the time, our writing would get very boring. We use compound sentences to link ideas and images together. For example:

I ate the apple (one simple sentence) *but* (conjunction) *I didn't eat the core* (one simple sentence).

'And', 'so', 'but', 'yet', 'or' and 'however' are the conjunctions or joining words that are used to make a compound sentence. A semi-colon may also be used.

A compound sentence is like two engines that are joined together. Just as two engines are more powerful than one, so two simple sentences give us more information.

1 **Put brackets around each simple sentence in the following compound sentences. For example: (My father comes home from work) and (he reads the newspaper).**

  a. The little girl put on a dress and she put on her shoes.

  b. Will you take the bus or do you want me to take you?

  c. The cat meowed all night so everyone slept badly.

  d. Dinosaurs are extinct but they are still popular.

  e. I am tired; I didn't get much sleep last night.

2 **Put the following sentences into compound sentences.**

  a. He entered the room. He did not sit down.

  _____

  b. The dog is large. He is kind.

  _____

  c. Mum is patient. She never gets angry.

  _____

ISBN: 9780170462983

d. I came home late. I am in trouble.

_____

e. The gauge says empty. We need to get petrol.

_____

3 Write down the compound sentence from the following paragraph.

> Zilla thought her name was strange. Her father had a fascination for names out of the ordinary. It didn't bother her much but she got sick of the teasing at school. She went through a stage of answering only to the name of Mary, much to the amusement of her family. But it lasted just three weeks, right about the time the new boy next door remarked that he thought her name was cool.

_____

_____

_____

4 Add a conjunction and a simple sentence to the following simple sentences to make a compound sentence. For example: *I love my shoes but they don't fit me.*

a. I love ice-cream _____

b. I struggle with maths _____

c. Reading books is okay _____

d. Last night was so hot _____

e. I want to be rich _____

5 Write down your own compound sentences.

a. _____

b. _____

c. _____

d. _____

e. _____

SPELLING TROUBLE-SHOOTING

There, their and they're

There is a word that shows you where someone or something is.
For example: *The exit is over **there**.*

Their is a word that tells you who owns it. For example: *It is **their** dog.*

They're is a contraction for 'they are'. For example: ***They're** going on holiday tomorrow.*

1 **Read the following sentences carefully putting** there, their **or** they're **in the space provided.**

a. Could you please put the shopping down over _____ .

b. The snails left _____ glistening trails on the deck.

c. I'm not sure where the scissors are. I think _____ in the top drawer.

d. I went to my cousin's house on Saturday; _____ swimming pool is a great place to cool off.

e. _____ were a lot of people in the queue for tickets. I hope _____ not all wanting to see the same movie as me!

Affect and effect

Affect is a verb, a doing word. A good way to remember is: **A** = **A**ction (verb). **A** = **Affect**. For example: *If I eat too much chocolate, it will **affect** me.* Meaning that it will do something to me.

Effect is a noun. It is the name of the result of an action. For example: *What is the effect of eating paint?* What is the result of eating paint? **E** = nam**e** (noun). **E** = r**e**sult.

2 **Read the following sentences carefully and circle, using red pen, the correct word to complete the sentence.**

a. The special effects/affects in the film *Star Wars: The Force Awakens* are excellent.

b. I was disappointed with the effect/affect of my studying.

c. Chewing my fingers effects/affects my nails.

d. My moaning had no effect/affect on my parents.

e. If I study hard it will effect/affect my results.

f. My teacher said the effect/affect of my giggling effected/affected the rest of the class.

Accept and except

Accept is a verb, a doing word. It means 'to receive'. A good way to remember is: **A** = **A**ction (verb). **A** = **A**ccept. For example: *I accept your invitation*. I **(do something to)** your invitation.

Except is a preposition. It means 'not including'. For example: *We all went to the movies, **except** Bronwyn*. We all went to the movies **(not including)** Bronwyn.

3   **Read the following and circle the correct word to complete each sentence.**

   a.   The elders accept/except the koha from the visitors.

   b.   I like all ice-cream accept/except chocolate.

   c.   The ewe did not accept/except her lamb.

   d.   The shop does not accept/except credit cards accept/except Visa.

   e.   Schools should accept/except all types of students accept/except drug dealers.

Your and you're

Your is a word that tells you who owns it. For example: *This is **your** dog*.

You're is a contraction for 'you are'. For example: ***You're** to come with me*.

4   **Read the following sentences carefully, putting your or you're in the space provided.**

   a.   _____ going to be in a lot of trouble when Mum gets home!

   b.   Have you brought _____ sweatshirt? It could get windy in the ranges.

   c.   Excuse me, is this _____ dog?

   d.   I am the leader of the Blue team. _____ in charge of the Yellow team.

   e.   _____ proofreading has improved tenfold since taking extra tuition.

Weather or whether

Weather is a noun. **Whether** is a conjunction (a joining word).

5   **Read the following sentences carefully, putting weather or whether in the space provided.**

   a.   This _____ is terrible: it is raining cats and dogs!

   b.   You need to decide _____ you are taking a pack or a suitcase with you.

   c.   I have always thought being a _____ presenter would be a good job.

   d.   The _____ forecast will determine if soccer is cancelled.

ISBN: 9780170462983

REVISION AND PRACTICE

Use a capital letter for ...

- The start of every new sentence.
- Using the word 'I'.
- Days of the week.
- Months of the year.
- Holidays.
- Important words in the titles of books, television programmes and films.

Use a full stop at ...

- The end of every sentence. We do this so that the reader has a moment to take in what the sentence has just said, and also to separate sentences so they make sense.

The comma is used to ...

- Put a sentence into parts, making the ideas easier to read.
- Separate items in a list.

The apostrophe is used to ...

- Show ownership.
- Show where letters are missed out in a contraction.

Speech marks are used to ...

- Show when someone has spoken. All punctuation marks that are part of the spoken words go inside the speech marks. All other punctuation marks go on the outside of the speech marks.

You use a new paragraph in your writing when ...

- There is a change of topic.
- There is a change of speaker.
- Time has passed.
- There is a change of place.
- There is a change of person.

ISBN: 9780170462983

Megan has just stolen some pies for her and Jeremy to eat. Jeremy is not happy about it but Megan doesn't see anything wrong with what she has done. They are travelling on the Interislander Cook Strait Ferry. Rewrite the following paragraph, putting in the correct punctuation. You may like to mark it in pencil first.

megan appeared carrying a greasy bag in one hand time for breakfast she said as she plonked herself down beside him i thought you might be hungry i am jeremy answered how much? nuffin megan said through a mouth filled with mince pie i borrowed it you stole it? man youre quick he pulled his pie out of the bag its not stealing in the literal sense of the word its not like well be taking anything off the ship what are you on about? were gonna be here for a few hours by that time this stuff would have gone through our digestive systems ... you are so disgusting! seriously we dont leave the boat with anything more than we came on

_____

_____

_____

_____

_____

_____

_____

_____

_____

_____

_____

_____

The publishers of this extract included the following. Beside each, write how many you used.

| capital letters | 19 _____ | full stops | 12 _____ | commas | 6 _____ |
| apostrophes | 6 _____ | speech marks | 24 _____ | | |

ISBN: 9780170462983

SIMILES

A simile is a phrase that compares two things, using 'like' or 'as'.

Similes are used by writers and poets to help us picture in our minds what they are writing about. We can think of similes as the writer trying to 'paint us a picture' or 'create a movie' in our heads.

A **simile** works by comparing two things and saying they have characteristics that are **similar**. For instance, you might read a sentence about a beautiful green field. It is hard to picture exactly what type of green it is. If the writer had also said the colour of the field was like a Granny Smith apple, you would have had a clearer picture of the colour.

A simile *always* uses either 'like' or 'as' to connect the two features being compared. For example:

*The car went by **as** fast **as** a cheetah.*

By using a thing we already know moves fast, a cheetah, we can picture exactly how quickly the car is moving. If 'cheetah' is replaced with the word 'snail', we get a completely different picture; that of a very slow car.

Some other examples of similes are:

*Missy sings **like** a nightingale.*

*Maia's long hair was **as** soft **as** silk.*

1 **Look carefully at the following sentences and show whether they are similes by circling either YES or NO.**

a.	The plants wore their flowers like jewellery.	YES	NO
b.	Carolyn's T-shirt was as yellow as the sun.	YES	NO
c.	The cold ice-cream sent an electric shock down my tooth.	YES	NO
d.	The little boy stood as straight as a soldier.	YES	NO
e.	The car was the colour of blood.	YES	NO

2 **Underline the similes in the following passage.**

Caitlin's smile was as wide as the sea. Her birthday had finally arrived! She raced down the stairs two at a time and headed for where she knew her presents would be. There they were, piled like a pyramid on the kitchen table. Her mother laughed at her excitement and pointed to the other side of the room where her father stood. In front of him was the one thing Caitlin had been wishing for – her first bike! It was as blue as the sky, with a rainbow of ribbons trailing from each handle. She rang the bell. It sounded like a happy angel. Never had she received a present like this!

ISBN: 9780170462983

3 If you listen carefully, you will hear people use similes every day. There are a lot of common sayings that are, in fact, similes. The exercise below requires you to think carefully about some of these sayings and complete the similes.

a. As _____ as a rose.

b. As _____ as an arrow.

c. As _____ as a lion.

d. As _____ as a mouse.

e. As _____ as a baby's bottom.

f. As _____ as a knife.

g. As _____ as a snail.

h. As _____ as the sky.

i. As _____ as a pancake.

j. As _____ as a fiddle.

k. As _____ as a mule.

l. As _____ as lightning.

4 Using the words in the box below complete the similes.

slow	ruby	hard	pink
ox	moon	strong	snail
concrete	red	round	candy floss

a. As _____ as an _____

b. As _____ as a _____

c. As _____ as a _____

d. As _____ as _____

e. As _____ as _____

f. As _____ as the _____

ISBN: 9780170462983

METAPHORS

A metaphor is where one thing is said to be another.

Now that you have similes under your belt, let's have a look at another technique writers use to 'paint us a picture'. The metaphor, like the simile, makes a comparison but it does not use the words 'like' or 'as'. Instead, a metaphor says that one thing **is** another. Confused? Have a look at the following examples.

If we were to use a simile to paint the colour of the sun, we would say:

*The sun is **like** a gold coin.*

If we were to use a metaphor, we would take out 'like' and say:

*The sun **is** a gold coin.*

Here is another example. The simile would say:

*The moon is **like** a golf ball hit high into the night sky.*

The metaphor would say:

*The moon **is** a golf ball hit high into the night sky.*

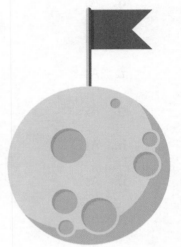

1 **Look carefully at the following sentences and show whether they are metaphors by circling either YES or NO.**

a.	The hose is a slippery snake that slithers across the lawn.	YES	NO
b.	The bed was as soft as a cotton ball.	YES	NO
c.	He was a taniwha in the board meeting.	YES	NO
d.	The wave is a dog rushing to the beach for its bone.	YES	NO
e.	It was as cold as a freezer on the mountain top.	YES	NO

2 **Underline the metaphors in the following passage.**

I lay in my backyard soaking up the sun, and, like a spy, investigated my surroundings.

The fence was a row of soldiers standing to attention around the perimeter. The washing

line whirled like a ferris wheel, the laundry, brightly coloured people enjoying the ride.

The hose slithered snake-like across the lawn while Cassius the cat stalked his unseen prey like

a lion in a far-off jungle.

3 **Take the following similes and, in the space provided, rewrite them as metaphors.**

a. The boat was like an island in the rolling sea.

_____

b. From the helicopter the fields looked like a patchwork quilt.

_____

c. My watch strap felt like a snake wrapped firmly around my wrist.

_____

d. Her eyes were like blazing pools of fire.

_____

e. The grapefruit is like the sun of the citrus fruit.

_____

4 **Now it is time for you to be a little creative! Below you will see a metaphor poem about the moon. It is made up of five metaphors. On the right-hand side you have room to write your own poem. You can use anything you like as your topic but, if you are stuck, why not choose the sun? You may like to plan your poem on a sheet of paper before you copy it tidily into your book.**

What is ... the Moon?

The moon is a golf ball

Hit high into the night sky.

It is a white dinner plate

On the tablecloth of darkness.

It is a Mint Imperial

That has rolled on to the navy carpet.

It is a blob of Twink

On a sheet of black paper.

It is a night-light

Glowing on the wall of a dark room.

What is ... the _____

The _____

_____

It is _____

_____

It is _____

_____

It is _____

_____

It is _____

_____

ISBN: 9780170462983

PERSONIFICATION

When a non-living thing is given living characteristics or when a non-human thing is given human characteristics, it is called personification.

Personification is a special kind of metaphor but this time the comparison needs to be between non-living or non-human objects or features and living or human objects or features. For instance:

*As I ran, the tree's gnarled **fingers** grabbed at my jacket.*

Here we have given the tree, a non-human object, the human characteristic or feature of having fingers.

Another example would be:

*The desert's **skin** was dry and wrinkled.*

Here the desert has been given the human characteristic of having skin as its surface.

Be careful you don't confuse personification and metaphor.

1 **Look carefully at the following sentences and say whether they show personification by circling either YES or NO.**

a.	The car's eyes shone as it approached the house.	YES	NO
b.	She was as wild as a winter storm.	YES	NO
c.	David's legs gave way like those of a young foal.	YES	NO
d.	Death's cold hand reached around her throat.	YES	NO
e.	The diamonds glistened like teardrops from her ears.	YES	NO

2 **Underline both the non-human object and the human characteristic in each of the following sentences.**

a. The bbq tongs snapped their jaws shut around the sausage.

b. The postie shoved the letters into the mouth of the mailbox and rode on.

c. The leaves danced as the wind wafted across the yard.

d. The baked bananas were sleeping in a bag of tin foil.

e. The zip's teeth closed as I did up my polar fleece for extra warmth.

ISBN: 9780170462983

3 Underline the personification in the following passage.

Isabella ran wildly through the dark night. She could feel the dampness of the air seeping into her clothing. The streetlights winked at her as the storm threatened to cut out their life source. She could feel the wind tearing at her skin, pulling at her jacket as she turned the corner into an alley. Her torch danced in the dark, searching erratically for a safe haven. A lone light called out to her at the end of the street. Could she trust this place?

4 For each of the following sentences, underline the human characteristic given to personify the word in bold type.

a. The **stream** chattered to the rocks as it rushed merrily by.

b. The **washing** danced around the line in time with the wind.

c. The **door handle** grabbed at my shirt as I ran past.

d. My **duvet** insisted on creeping down the bed in the middle of the night.

e. The **wind** roared at the **trees** standing guard on the coastline.

5 You can use personification to bring anything to life. Below is a list of everyday household items. Have a go at writing sentences to personify them.

a. Vacuum cleaner

_____

_____

b. Toaster

_____

_____

c. Blow-drier

_____

_____

d. Broom

_____

_____

ISBN: 9780170462983

ALLITERATION

Alliteration is the repetition of consonant sounds, usually at the beginning of words, in a sequence or phrase.

We have just spent time looking at how writers paint a picture for us by using words. The next set of techniques is used by writers to put a soundtrack to their passage. The simile, metaphor and personification help us to *see* what is happening, while alliteration, onomatopoeia, assonance and rhyme help us either to *hear* what is happening or to *create* an atmosphere or mood.

Alliteration occurs when there is a sequence of words that begins with, or has in them, the same letter. Alliteration commonly occurs in tongue twisters. For example:

Peter **P**iper **p**icked a **p**eck of **p**ickled **p**eppers.

And another one:

*How mu**ch** woo**d** **c**oul**d** a **w**oodchu**ck** **ch**u**ck** if a **w**oodchu**ck** **c**oul**d** **ch**u**ck** woo**d**?*

Why use alliteration? Well, there are several reasons. The first is that it helps draw our attention to a line of a poem or a particular image the writer thought was important. Another reason is that it can both slow down our reading or speed up the words in order to create an atmosphere. Advertisements often use alliteration to make things easy to remember.

1 **Underline the alliteration in the following sentences. Then, in the box, write the letter that is being used in the alliteration.**

a. Tatiana took ten attempts to touch the top. ☐

b. Hercules heaved the huge giant over his head. ☐

c. Silly Sally shook the sausage at the skinny scoundrel. ☐

d. The frog frolicked freely in the lily pads. ☐

e. Pita purchased a pencil, pad and paperclips from Whitcoulls. ☐

f. On Wednesday we saw a wētā while hanging out washing on the line. ☐

2 **Words have been left out of the following sentences. Using the words in the box and, ensuring you keep the alliteration consistent, complete each sentence.**

blue	*Street*	knitting	Serious
nimble	cabbage	bike	climbed
starts	cautious	never-ending	seven
needles	silently	knitted	swimming

ISBN: 9780170462983

a. Benjamin rode his _____ to the barbecue.

b. *Shortland* _____ _____ strictly at _____ .

c. _____ Sam sat _____ watching the _____ .

d. Nana _____ _____ scarfs with her

_____ _____ .

e. The _____ cat _____ carefully up the _____ tree.

3   **Using the words given, form a sentence that shows alliteration. You will have to add your own words, of course!**

    a.   swiftly, sailed, sea: _____

_____

_____

    b.   darted, dolphins, deck, daintily: _____

_____

_____

    c.   fly, frequently, flew: _____

_____

_____

    d.   Paul, sunbathed, postcard, Puerto Rico, surfed, swum:

_____

_____

_____

4   **Alliteration is used frequently in magazines and newspapers. Grab a selection of publications and cut sentences out from headlines, captions or adverts that display alliteration. Try to get at least three words that give the alliteration. Once you have found two or three, tidily glue or tape them into the empty space around the edges of this page.**

ONOMATOPOEIA

Onomatopoeia is when the sound of the word imitates or suggests the meaning or noise of the action described.

Sometimes these words are called 'sound words'. As the definition suggests, they are words that have been made up to sound like, or echo, the action they make. They are words such as *snap*, *crackle* and *pop* or *ping*, *pitter* and *patter*.

Poets use sound words a lot because they help the reader to experience what is happening by recalling the sound that something makes and thereby improving our ability to understand what is going on.

1 **Underline the sound words in the following sentences.**

a. The clock went 'tick, tick, tick'.

b. The boom of the cannon could be heard throughout the park.

c. The little dog yapped at the postman's ankles as he went by.

d. The bird chirped from its house at the top of the tree.

e. 'Woosh!' Dad, the wonder chef, had set fire to the sausages.

f. The soft-drink can fizzed as I pulled the tab.

2 **From the box, choose the sound word that best completes each sentence.**

thud	slop	tapped	ouch	sizzle	bang

a. The drummer made a huge _____ on his bass drum.

b. The _____ of the steaks on the barbecue made our mouths water.

c. I could hear the water _____ against the side of the boat.

d. The potatoes fell off the bench with an almighty _____

e. The shoes of the street dancer _____ on the pavement.

f. My brother said _____ at least a hundred times as he crossed

the prickle-infested lawn.

ISBN: 9780170462983

3 You will often need to find onomatopoeia while reading a poem. Carefully read the poem *Stormy Sailing* and underline all the onomatopoeic words you can find.

Stormy Sailing
The water crashed against the deck.
My raincoat squelched and oozed with water
as I heaved against the heavy helm.
A drip,
   drip,
      drip,
         fell from my nose
as lightning cracked and seagulls screeched.
Stays twanged and pinged against the mast
as we dove off the top of the waves like
a springboard diver in the Olympics.
The sea was grey and the swell alive
And that's just how I like it.

4 Now try to think of your own sound words. In the space provided write a word that would represent the appropriate noise or action.

a. a tennis ball being hit

b. a happy cat

c. a person bellyflopping into a pool

d. walking in mud with gumboots on

e. the sound of an earthquake

f. someone eating soup

g. a cricket ball going through a window

h. a rooster crowing

5 Take your pencil and book outside, find a comfortable position and write down as many sounds as you can hear by coming up with a suitable sound word.

Description of Sound		Sound Word
	=	
	=	
	=	

ISBN: 9780170462983

ASSONANCE

Assonance is the deliberate repetition of the same vowel sound followed by a different consonant sound.

Assonance is one of the most difficult techniques that this book will deal with, so listen up! Assonance is a sound technique that is usually found in poetry and because poetry was traditionally meant to be read aloud you would normally *hear* the assonance. When we try to find assonance we are looking at the vowel and consonant sounds. Vowels are, of course, a, e, i, o and u, while consonant sounds are all the other letters of the alphabet.

An example of assonance is:

> A *stitch* in *time* saves *nine*.

Hear how the words **time** and **nine** both have the vowel sound **i** as their dominant sound?
But for assonance, they must have different consonants following – one has **m** after the vowel while the other one has **n**.

Some people like to say assonance creates a musical effect while others say that it is used to highlight imagery. Both comments are correct. When looking for assonance, it might help if you read the passage aloud to yourself so that you can hear the sounds. Do not let your eyes deceive you!

1 **Underline the assonance in the following sentences.**

   a. Rebecca sleeps neatly in the bed.

   b. The boat was soaked with water.

   c. I like ice-cream.

   d. The ape ate his banana.

   e. I went through the blue door.

2 **Now they get a bit harder! Try these ones, again underlining the assonance.**

   a. The fire flickered shyly in the hearth.

   b. Max cheated in the beep test.

   c. I lost two shoes on the field.

   d. Stuart always knew what to do.

   e. They were further away than that yesterday.

ISBN: 9780170462983

RHYME

Rhyme is the repetition of similar sounds, usually at the ends of lines.

Rhyme is another technique that creates sound patterns. It is mostly used in order to be pleasing to the ear and to give a piece of writing rhythm and flow. Rhyme is also used to hold certain lines of poetry together in order to link ideas and images.

1 **Join the words that rhyme by linking them together with a line.**

spent	pose
dog	mask
hose	can
coat	pen
man	bent
Ben	boat
cask	bog

2 **Link the words that rhyme in each of the following verses by joining them together with a line.**

a. My mother is nice

My mother is kind

When I eat ice

She does not mind.

b. I love the sun

I love to sail

I especially have fun

When the wind's from the tail.

c. When I get home from school

I leap into the pool

I swim really well

Which I think is just swell.

3 **The simplest rhymes of all are those you will find in children's books. Look through any books that belong to either you or a younger brother or sister for one that rhymes. You could try Dr. Seuss or nursery rhymes and read them out loud to hear the sound the rhyme makes.**

ISBN: 9780170462983

REVISION

This exercise has been designed to test how much you have learnt about poetic techniques. Read back over the section before you begin.

A Day at the Beach

Car doors slam and children cheer,
Our day at the beach has just begun.
The sun, like the colour of summer corn
Spreads its arms wide to give us warmth.
While the beach is a patchwork quilt,
Umbrellas and towels covering the sand.
The pōhutukawa blooms red
Gracefully offering us shade under
Its thick umbrella of leaves.
Suntan lotion is slopped and slapped
As shirts slip off and togs slip up.
There's the whooping of children racing
After bright beach balls
And the lapping of waves, their fingers
Trying to catch hold of our feet.
Parents relax, nose in a book,
Children play; all are there to enjoy the day.
As the sun bows farewell and the water recedes
We pack up our gear and, like ants,
File singly back to the car.
The day has ended as the gulls screech their goodbyes.
I dream of when I'll next be by the sea's side.

ISBN: 9780170462983

Read the poem carefully and find examples of the following poetic techniques.

1 **Simile**

Example One: _____

Example Two: _____

2 **Metaphor**

Example One: _____

Example Two: _____

3 **Personification**

Example One: _____

Example Two: _____

4 **Alliteration**

Example One: _____

Example Two: _____

5 **Onomatopoeia**

Example One: _____

Example Two: _____

6 **Assonance**

Example One: _____

Example Two: _____

EXTRA PRACTICE 1

1 **Identify the** parts of speech **in the following passage.**

> We were beachcombing, me and Robbie, because Grandad had said that his beach was excellent for finding things washed up from the liners and cruise ships that pass by. That the current was just right to bring in interesting stuff.
>
> We'd started slowly down the south end of the beach near the twisted pōhutukawa because Grandad said that was the best place – it was kind of like a settling pool for the currents. Robbie found a pair of child's glasses; I found a munted Frisbee.
>
> We kept along the high tide mark but we swept down toward the water every now and then. About two thirds of the way along the beach, we found her.

a. Common noun (find 5) _____

b. Proper noun (find 2) _____

c. Pronoun (find 5) _____

d. Adjective (find 3) _____

e. Verb (find 3) _____

f. Auxiliary verb (find 1) _____

g. Adverb (find 1) _____

h. Conjunction (find 2) _____

i. Preposition (find 3) _____

2 **Correct all the** punctuation errors **in the following sentence.**

> well he asked pulling the hood of his cloak tightly over his nose to avoid being overwhelmed by the stench from the cauldron and the moist hot air of the dirty hut

_____

_____

_____

_____

3 **Identify the** type of sentences **used in the following paragraph. Simple or Compound?**

> [1]Ice lined the footpath and the concrete cracked and crumbled under her shoes. [2]I should have worn boots.
> Crunch. [3]She came to a halt. [4]She turned her head slowly and regarded the house at the end of the drive with no small amount of anxiety. [5]Her hands twisted nervously inside the double pocket of her hooded jersey.

1. _____

2. _____

3. _____

4. _____

5. _____

4 **Read the sentences and choose the correct word from each of the underlined words.**

a. It's/Its supposed to be fine today. A plague on this weather/whether.

b. Because there/they're/there is a rain storm, tennis is off.

c. Mum says Dad's snoring affects/effects how much sleep she gets. Shame!

d. I got all my stationery accept/except the graphic calculator.

e. You're/Your going to love your/you're new teacher!

f. Weather/Whether you choose to do art or not, I still want you to keep up with music.

g. I chose not to accept/except the allegations that I was unfair.

h. There/They're/Their always telling everyone how fab they are.

i. I am so affected/effected by my brother's news, I have to spend some time in reflection.

j. There/They're/Their ideas for the social were interesting.

EXTRA PRACTICE 2

1 **Identify the** parts of speech **in the following passage.**

> A heavy shower of rain splattered against the blackened windscreen, blurring the streetlights and creating an eerie, incandescent glow. Emma flicked a glossy red nail and her wipers quickly spun into action, whirring as she skidded around the curve.

a. Common noun (find 5) _____

b. Proper noun (find 1) _____

c. Pronoun (find 2) _____

d. Adjective (find 3) _____

e. Verb (find 3) _____

f. Adverb (find 1) _____

g. Conjunction (find 1) _____

h. Preposition (find 2) _____

2 **Correct all the** punctuation errors **in the following passage.**

> as one the three strange women turned from the blackened pot cooking over a fire each of them held a wooden cup the eldest of the three stepped forward the flickering light from the fire deepening the craggy lines in her face and lifted her cup to him speak she demanded

_____

_____

_____

_____

_____

_____

ISBN: 9780170462983   PHOTOCOPYING OF THIS PAGE IS RESTRICTED UNDER LAW.

3 Using a red pen, write the missing apostrophes in the passage below.

> Its not fair! Youre always on Mums computer. Im suppose to finish my maths homework by tonight and its on her hard drive. You shouldve asked first. Why dont you go to Matts house and play your games on his computer?

4 Read the sentences and choose the correct word from each of the underlined words.

a. I put my book over there/they're/their and now it's gone.

b. 'What were the affects/effects of the extra tutoring?' my teacher asked.

c. He was too busy to accept/except the prize – a trip to Australia!

d. Have you remembered to bring you're/your togs?

e. The party was ruined because of the weather/whether.

f. Everyone was at the beach accept/except the non-swimmers.

g. The students are going to have there/they're/their lunch in the dining hall.

h. My teasing had no affect/effect on my brother's bad mood.

i. I can't work out weather/whether I'm supposed to take five subjects or six.

j. There/They're/Their always chatty in maths and it drives the teacher nuts.

EXTRA PRACTICE 3

1 Identify the parts of speech in the following passage.

'What's that?' Robbie asked, pointing to a fleshy lump huddled amongst the rocks. 'Looks like a body.'

My stomach squeezed. I wasn't in the mood to find a dead, rotting body on the beach. 'We should go get Grandad,' I told him. 'Probably best to have an adult around.'

'Don't be a sissy,' Robbie said, giving me one of his looks. My little brother can be really tough sometimes and I knew that this was his way of reminding me, though I was the first born son, he was stronger and tougher than me – even if he was two years younger and three inches shorter.

a. Common noun (find 5) _____

_____

b. Proper noun (find 2) _____

c. Abstract noun (find 2) _____

d. Pronoun (find 4) _____

e. Adjective (find 5) _____

_____

f. Verb (find 5) _____

_____

g. Auxiliary verb (find 3) _____

h. Adverb (find 1) _____

i. Conjunction (find 2) _____

2 Correct all the punctuation and spelling errors in the following sentence.

the wipers swished sluggishly backwards and forewards across the windscreen it was cold and the wet whether that had nagged at them all the way from auckland started to irritate even Sophies borrowed army-issue overcoat could not keep her warm she was miserable

_____

_____

_____

_____

ISBN: 9780170462983

3 In the space provided, identify which type of imagery is being used. Is it simile, metaphor, or personification?

a. The sky was angry. ....

b. This holiday I was determined that everybody
   will be happy like sweet tooths in a lolly factory. ....

c. He was a volcano ready to explode! ....

d. It was dark, the movie was starting.
   The popcorn beckoned and the polar
   fleece blanket hugged me. ....

e. Matua Pete was a mule as he wouldn't
   change his ways for anything. ....

f. The pines swayed like ships in a storm. ....

g. The book snapped shut as it fell to the floor. ....

h. His beady eyes flicked around the room
   like a meerkat on patrol. ....

4 Read the sentences and choose the correct word from each of the underlined words.

a. We have a <u>creak/creek</u> at the bottom of our paddock.

b. You need to go <u>threw/through</u> the door at the end of the corridor to get to the canteen.

c. She has an important new job as the college <u>principle/principal</u>.

d. After her illness she looked very <u>pail/pale</u>.

e. Don't let the rest of your sandwich go to <u>waste/waist</u>.

f. My friend <u>sent/cent</u> me some chocolates.

g. <u>Your/you're</u> books must be covered by the end of the week or <u>your/you're</u> going to receive a detention.

h. I love to go on the lawn in my <u>bear/bare</u> feet.

i. What a breathtaking <u>scene/seen</u> the mountains are.

j. The window <u>pane/pain</u> has chipped paint.

EXTRA PRACTICE 4

1 **Identify the** parts of speech **in the following passage.**

> The car lurched violently, and Sophie watched in horror the headlights pointing into nothing but sleeting rain as the car tumbled over a bank. The force of their fall pushed them both hard against their seats and apart from someone's screaming, there was no noise at all.

a. Common noun (find 5) _____

b. Proper noun (find 1) _____

c. Pronoun (find 2) _____

d. Adjective (find 1) _____

e. Verb (find 3) _____

f. Adverb (find 1) _____

g. Conjunction (find 2) _____

h. Preposition (find 2) _____

2 **Correct all the** punctuation **and** spelling errors **in the following passage.**

> ive never liked swiming just cant seem to relax in the water its as if im always fighting to get my breath and I just never learnt how to dive its pretty hard to look cool if you have to lower yourself carefuly down the side of the pool while every one else is doing olympic-style dives their bodies braking the surface of the water like arrows

_____

_____

_____

_____

_____

_____

_____

ISBN: 9780170462983

Using a red pen, punctuate the following with speech marks, commas and full stops to make the meaning clear.

a. I guess it's a very individual thing she says When you see someone wearing a tā moko you wonder if that's what represents them. Does it say something important about who they are?

b. But I don't want to go home yet wailed Anna to her aunt I know Anna but this is the easiest for everyone

c. Would you like cracked pepper with your soup? the waiter asked

d. The tourist stood in the Octagon Excuse me? he asked a couple of kids with skateboards Can you point me in the direction of the railway station?

e. My favourite foods are bananas apples and peaches she told the interviewer But I'm also partial to a nice piece of chocolate cake

 Read the sentences and choose the correct word from each of the underlined words

a. Our game is dependent on the weather/whether doing the right thing.

b. There/They're/Their always late to Taekwondo.

c. If only my homework didn't affect/effect how much time I have to chillax!

d. I paid for everything accept/except the drinks.

e. You're/Your heading to town with you're/your wallet?

f. Weather/Whether our kapa haka team wins or loses, we are still champs.

g. He was not present so could not accept/except his award.

h. I put the essay over there/they're/their; on the teacher's desk.

i. I am so sick of the affect/effect Daylight Saving has on my mornings.

j. The parking warden said that there/they're/their cars were parked illegally.

FINAL TEST

Work carefully through this test. There is no time limit so there is no need to rush.

1   **Identify the parts of speech in the following sentence.**
Write one example in the spaces below.

> General Blake made the squad of young army men stand to attention.
> However, they were being disobedient and ran quickly away to sit on the hill.

    a. Common noun   _____

    b. Proper noun   _____

    c. Collective noun   _____

    d. Abstract noun   _____

    e. Pronoun   _____

    f. Adjective   _____

    g. Verb   _____

    h. Adverb   _____

    i. Conjunction   _____

    j. Preposition   _____

2   **Identify the parts of speech in the following sentence.**
Write one example in the spaces below.

> Before long, the men realised that to get all the flock of sheep in the square pen,
> they would have to tempt them sneakily with Pascall marshmallows and milk.

    a. Common noun   _____

    b. Proper noun   _____

    c. Collective noun   _____

    d. Pronoun   _____

    e. Adjective   _____

    f. Verb   _____

    g. Auxilary verb   _____

    h. Adverb   _____

    i. Conjunction   _____

    j. Preposition   _____

ISBN: 9780170462983   PHOTOCOPYING OF THIS PAGE IS RESTRICTED UNDER LAW.

3 Correct all the punctuation and spelling errors in the following sentences.

a. my name is seung and i live in auckland i like apples pears bananas and grapes

b. i crashed my fathers car because i was watching the dog trip over its lead

c. youre house is in wellington our's is in christchurch where bird's fly north for the winter and where dad says you cant go to the beach

d. the boys pencil case was left there with his friends bags and there pencil cases

e. usually in the evening when the sky is red he explained the following day is fine but he went on thats not what well rely on ill go ring the met service thats my grandfather ted hes the practical sort

ISBN: 9780170462983

4 **Identify two simple and two compound sentences in the following paragraph.**

You must answer all the questions. This test is a difficult one but you can do it if you go carefully. Read over all that you have done and check your work is correct. It's that simple. Try not to look at the answer.

a. Simple

_____

Simple

_____

b. Compound

_____

Compound

_____

5 **Read the following paragraph. Then, in the spaces below, write one example of each of the identified poetic terms.**

The heat of the day still hung heavily in the air, reluctant to let go of its grasp. Behind us, the bach sat silent, dark, waiting for us to bring in our noise and mess like unruly children let into a classroom. We tramped up the dusty dunes, beach gear jangling against our bodies, backs burnt and bruised from a long day swimming and climbing and playing.

And now, with the sound of the waves booming in the distance, we enter our haven, sighing and pleased. What a wonderful day. It had been sheer heaven.

a. Simile

_____

b. Metaphor

_____

c. Personification

_____

d. Alliteration

_____

e. Assonance

_____

f. Onomatopoeia

_____

Total

ISBN: 9780170462983   PHOTOCOPYING OF THIS PAGE IS RESTRICTED UNDER LAW.